# Filled to Spill

## by Barbara Arbo

FILLED TO SPILL
ISBN # 0-9710450-2-X
© 2005 Barbara Arbo

Published by:
Arbo Ministries
PO Box 8552
Fort Worth, TX 76124-0552
1-800-276-ARBO

# TABLE OF CONTENTS

# DEDICATION

I would like to dedicate this book to Pastor Bob and Joy Nichols, founders of Calvary Cathedral, International in Ft. Worth, Texas. Their passionate and transparent hunger for revival inspires me to seek God with all my heart, and be revived again and again, with the purpose of reaching others with God's love and power.

# ACKNOWLEDGEMENTS

I would also like to say thank you with all my heart to the special relationships in my life that God has placed there, to share my dreams and help make them a reality. Thank you Betsy Stanton for the cover artwork, Barbara Pendleton for your computer skills in typeset and design, Frat'Antonio @San Giorgio Studios for catching my vision for "pot" icons and my daughter-in-law Jennifer Arbo whose knowledge of literary do's and don'ts (besides her love for my son) makes her a great blessing to me!

# PREFACE

This book was conceived in 1991, following an intense encounter with God in my own life that revived me. I saw God move miraculously to pour out His Spirit, filling the church with the richest measure of His divine presence.

I recall so many people at the time who didn't understand the strange manifestations of weeping, laughing, running, shaking, and even being stuck to the floor! My heart cried, in the midst of my own fresh touch, for the hearts of others to open and receive a fresh infilling of the Holy Ghost.

In God's wisdom, He saw that there was more that I needed to see. I've followed this river of God around the corner and down the bend, and see it today spilling into an ocean of humanity. I understand now that God's purpose of filling is all about spilling.

I trust that you will see a greater sense of purpose in the outpouring of God's Spirit and return often to drink from the river of God, staying ever-filled and ever-stimulated with the power of the Holy Spirit.

—Barbara Arbo

# FOREWORD

*"You let the distress bring you to God, not drive you from Him. The result was all gain, no loss. Distress that drives us to God does just that. It turns us around. It gets us back in the way of salvation. We never regret that kind of pain. But those who let distress drive them away from God are full of regrets and end up on a deathbed of regrets. And now, isn't it wonderful all the ways in which this distress has goaded you closer to God? You're more alive, more concerned, more sensitive, more reverent, more human, more passionate, more responsible. Looked at from any angle, you've come out of this with purity of heart."*
—II Corinthians 7:9-11 THE MESSAGE BIBLE


In 1990, I came face to face with the end of myself and realized I was dying inside. I felt under so much pressure, trying so hard to be God's woman of faith and power, and I was failing miserably. I had hired myself on as Executive Secretary to the Holy Ghost and believed I was doing a marvelous job taking care of all the little details of peoples' lives. No need to bother the Boss with these issues. After all, I could take care of it. I exhausted myself for hours night and day moving at top speed, doing my best to fix everyone's life around me. I was convinced that I had a gift in discerning what was wrong in others. I'd then get to work with the right tools of books, tapes, counseling, and hands-on ministry in working to fix their lives.

In the midst of this, I heard the Lord say, "Barbara, if you are so good at fixing people, why aren't you perfected yet?" Then He fired me from my position as Executive Secretary and told me I was to spend my energies seeking Him.

About this time, I had been diagnosed with a stomach full of ulcers with the root cause being worry and stress and it was suggested that I talk with a minister. Talk with a minister? I was one! I was so desperate for a touch from God. I needed to be healed and much more. I was down for the count and gasping for breath, desperate to be revived.

The simplest definition of revival I know is: "God comes," and truly, God came to me, and with a breath of fresh air, He revived me. When I cried out to Him in my distress, He answered me, but He didn't come in the way I had anticipated. I had that all figured out, too. I thought He would probably call me out in a church service with a word of knowledge, or perhaps I would be slain in the Spirit and His soothing balm of Gilead would coat my insides, healing me of my pain. Instead, I experienced a divine visitation that knocked me off my feet and left me sobbing at the altar so uncontrollably that I was sure people would think my husband had been abusing me! I was embarrassed at my lack of control, and even more so as I remained inebriated with His power and my mourning turned to joy. I was laughing without inhibition as He lifted the burdens off my shoulders and set me free.

In mere moments in His presence, God did in me what I could not do in myself or others — He brought change! Not only was I healed that night from a stomach of ulcers, but I was set free from the root of care and worry that had caused them. My desperation drove me to His presence, and in His presence I found fullness of joy. God came and I was revived!

He will do the same for you...if you seek Him, you will find Him, when you search for Him with all your heart.

# CHAPTER ONE

# DESPERATION

Are you looking for a way out, or a way in?

*"We are hedged in (pressed) on every side (troubled and oppressed in every way, but not cramped or crushed); we suffer embarrassments and are per-plexed and unable to find a way out, but not driven to despair...Assured that He who raised the Lord Jesus will raise us up also and bring us along with you into His presence."*
—II Corinthians 4:8, 14 AMP

*"You will show me the path of life; in Your presence is fullness of joy at Your right hand there are pleas-ures evermore."*
—Psalm 16:11 AMP

I am convinced that we don't need the relief of being out of our despair as much as we need the motivation to get into the presence of God. There is something about desperation, as distasteful as it is, that brings us to the end of ourselves, and there we find the beginning of God. Paul experienced this in Asia, when in II Corinthians 1:8-11 he graphically expresses his despair *"even of life itself...Indeed we felt within ourselves the sentence of death...BUT that was to keep us from trusting in and depending on ourselves instead of on the God who raises the dead." (AMP)*

Through the years, I have read several books on revival, the move of God, and the powerful signs and wonders demonstrated through revivalists of times past and today. The common thread I found in all of their lives was first of all desperation, and then a turning of their hearts to God in prevailing prayer. They were not just seeking a way out of their desperation, but the way in to Him, where they would experience the power of His resurrection.

John Alexander Dowie was pastoring a church in Sydney, Australia just before the turn of the twentieth century. He was affected by the plague that had broken out which caused him to have to bury thirty-four members of his congregation. He found himself desperately seeking God. God, ever faithful, brought him into the revelation of Acts 10:38 *"How God anointed Jesus of Nazareth with the Holy Ghost and with power: Who went about doing good, and healing all that were oppressed of the devil; for God was with Him (KJV)."* From that day on, not one more member of his congregation died from the plague. He then went on to launch a healing ministry in America that profoundly affected the healing revival!

Maria Woodworth Etter desperately sought God after she buried five of her six children. In seeking God, she had a vision that changed her life. Her vision became reality and soon revival broke out everywhere she went. For miles around, people were struck down by the power of God. At one point she went into a three-day trance during which continual miracles took place. Out of her ministry, a number of successful evangelists, pastors and teachers were raised up.

Charles Parham, healed from childhood rheumatic fever, was determined to see the God Who is the same yesterday, today, and forever. In October of 1900, he fasted and prayed and rented an old mansion in Topeka, Kansas, to start a Bible school. During a watch-night service on New Years, entering into 1901, he and others prayed, praised, and cried out to God. One woman, Agnes Ozmun asked for prayer to be filled with the Holy Spirit and spoke in, or wrote in Chinese for three days, non-stop! Miracles and healing took place so radically that they were evicted and driven to Houston, Texas where they started another school. This was the same school where William Seymour, a black man, blind in one eye from childhood smallpox, was so hungry and desperate for God that he sat outside the doors because of racial segregation. Even there he received the deposit of God's anointing that led him to accept the call to ministry and eventually was led to Azuza Street where God poured out His Spirit on all races alike. Statistics in 1990 showed that more than 370 million people had been affected by that outpouring of the Spirit.

There are more stories that could be told, but let's stop and talk about you and me. Are we the men and women that God is preparing to carry revival in this hour? Are we crying out to Him to take us into His plans and purposes, to stretch us, change us, and purge us of anything that could hinder His revival in us? We know God has promised to cover this earth with His glory, and I believe He's going to fill us, and then through us, spill that glory all around.

If you are desperate today, run to God, not from Him. He has made a secret place for you to come and find refuge, to see His strength made perfect, complete, and overflowing in your weakness. Let Him deliver you into a greater anointing and hunger for Him than you have ever had before!

Paul recognized in II Corinthians 1:10, *"for it is He that hath delivered and rescued us, it is He who will still rescue and save us, and on Him we set our hopes."* We too need to recognize that we have been delivered, will yet be delivered and are right now in the process of deliverance. After all, salvation is daily deliverance from sin's dominion.

To have a heart for God like David did, we need to face the heartache of discovering ourselves. My pastor used to say that the most difficult part of trials is that they show you who you really are, and that is not always attractive. If we recognize that we are powerless to change ourselves, only then will we be motivated to press into the Greater One to do in us that which we cannot do in ourselves.

> *"[NOT in your own strength] for it is God Who is ALL THE WHILE effectually at work in you [energizing and creating in you the power and desire] both to will and to work for His good pleasure and satisfaction and delight."*
> —Philippians 2:13 AMP (Emphasis added)

When we yield ourselves over to Him, He can accomplish the task of changing our hearts and cause us to hunger from within for Him.

For several months now, I have felt a craving. This may sound like a strange analogy, but when I suffered from stomach ulcers, it felt like something eating my insides, and something was! Worry and anxiety were the cause of that discomfort and the only thing that relieved it was God's healing and delivering power. Today, I don't have the pain of ulcers, and as a matter of fact, upon examination, they don't see any sign that I've ever even had an ulcer. Now I have a new feeling inside of me: I have a craving, an appetite, a hunger and a passion for Him that nothing else can satisfy. It eats at me, it challenges me to be less busy and more in fellowship with Him, it woos me to eternal things, it provokes me to look in the mirror of God's Word and see myself as He sees me—a mighty woman of faith and power able to submit the frailties and inadequacies of my flesh that can be seen in my natural mirror into His hands to be transformed.

In this hour, we are traveling on the path that God has prepared since the foundation of the world. The path is growing narrower, and there is not nearly the room for carts and baggage that we once carried with us. The culmination of all things is at hand. We desperately need God to do something new in us. *"Behold, I am doing a new thing! Now it springs forth; do you not perceive and know it and will you not give heed to it?"* (Isaiah 43:19 AMP)

For many years I lived in New England and enjoyed the historical villages that reenact the lifestyles of those who traveled to America on the Mayflower. It made me value even more our forefathers who boldly stepped out on the waters to seek the liberty and freedom to which they knew God called them. We realize that they were driven by a force bigger than natural wind, the winds of the Holy Spirit. Those winds were blowing and they could choose to resist and hide inside the secure houses of tradition, or they could go with the flow, following the promptings, throwing caution to the wind, to know God in all His multi-faceted personality.

We, too, are at the crossroads. Will we open our hearts and lives to the winds of God? Will we turn our hearts again to Him?

> *"So repent (change your mind and purpose); turn around and return [to God], that your sins may be erased (blotted out, wiped clean), that times of refreshing (of recovering from the effects of heat, of reviving with fresh air) may come from the presence of the Lord."*
>
> —Acts 3:19 AMP

Isaiah 55:6 says to seek the Lord while He may be found, to call upon Him while He is near, to seek Him as your first and most vital need. God has drawn near to His people, and is waiting for our response to draw near to Him. He is visiting today! As stated earlier, a simple definition of revival is "God comes." When He shows up at your door, will you make room for Him? Do you already have your plans so settled that His arrival is an unnerving interruption to you? Have you become so comfortable with your church's style of worship, that when a new song comes you don't like its intrusion? Are you so formatted with the program that God's intervention in the course of things throws you completely off course? Are you still leaving roasts in the oven every Sunday, hoping you'll be home by noon? Remember, it is God who prearranged your pathway. It is He that prepared a good life for you. God's part is to initiate revival. Our part is to respond to it.

In January of 1994, God gave me a vision showing me that the move of God in these last days would be like an elevator moving in a high-rise building, 24 hours a day. He said that every floor on which you could get off in this high-rise would be another degree of His glory. II Corinthians 3:18 says that we are changed from one degree of glory after another. He also showed me how wonderful every floor or degree of His glory is. None was better than the other, just fitting for a time or season or purpose. There isn't any greater degree of God's glory than healing when you've been sick, or deliverance if you've been tormented by the devil.

He further showed me how people would enjoy all the facets of His glory in these last days. They would be so excited and free. They would get off at different floors, thinking they'd arrived at the top floor. Some would believe that praise was the ultimate glory, others prayer, and some would be dancing and laughing with the Holy Ghost on the thirtieth floor thinking you hadn't experienced anything until you'd been there. Others who were weeping on the fourteenth floor, sharing the cleansing they'd just received would think that there was nothing more exhilarating. He said "It is all wonderful, for I make all things beautiful in My time!"

Then I saw mobs of people in the lobby waiting for the elevator. Some stood by, while others randomly kept pushing the button and waiting, but the elevator didn't seem to come. He showed me that we, as the people of God, push the button of God when we praise and when we pray. Psalm 22:3 says that God inhabits the praise of His people.

> *"And it shall come to pass, that before they call, I will answer; and while they are yet speaking, I will hear."*
> —Isaiah 65:24 KJV

Sometimes, as in any high-rise, we push the button and two minutes go by, five minutes, maybe a week or a month in your prayer life, and nothing shows up. Sometimes you find yourself pushing the button again and again trying to make the elevator show up faster! The good news is that it is inevitable that the elevator will show up, just as God will if you keep pressing in to Him. The important part is that when the elevator door opens, there is just one thing left for you to do: get on the elevator and go!

When it comes to revival and the move of God in this hour, if you have been crying out to God for His move, when He shows up go with Him! He will take you to those higher places that have been prepared for you. Whatever you do, don't stand in the lobby and stare at the door!

God has made provision to meet your every need and when the door opens you must step into the refreshing! Don't look around at everybody as if to say, "Do you suppose that this is the elevator door?" Romans 8:14 says that those that are led by the Spirit, they are the sons and daughters of God. Our spirit should bear witness with the Spirit of God. John 14:16-17 says that the world does not recognize the Holy Spirit, but we do! The sons of Issachar were discerning and recognized the times and seasons of God. Daniel recognized the hour of God's visitation and responded by seeking God. If we recognize that God is moving in this hour, you and I need to respond and seek the Lord.

Revival is God's heart reaching out to His people to refresh and strengthen them. Don't miss the days of His divine visitation. In His presence is fullness of joy, and that joy will be our strength to fulfill His purpose though us to our generation.

We must invite the Holy Spirit into our lives and make Him welcome. He will come where invited and abide where He is welcome. Urge Him to visit you. Entreat Him to stay. You can let the Father know without saying a word, whether He is welcome or not. You've had lots of practice when company comes to the door. Have you ever kept your door half shut, extending only your hand to receive whatever they brought; and, with a quick "thank you," let them know that now is not a good time for a visit? Perhaps you're busy with other things or not dressed for company and didn't answer the door. When God knocks, will you fling the door open wide, welcoming Him even if unexpected, urging Him to "please come in," and entreat Him to stay?

# CHAPTER TWO

# REVIVAL: A PRETTY PICTURE

*"... the time is coming when the earth shall be filled with the knowledge of the glory of the Lord as the waters cover the sea."*
—Habakkuk 2:14 AMP

It's time to make room for God in this hour. Stop focusing on the things that are desperate in your life and press into His presence. As the old hymn says, "Turn your eyes upon Jesus and the things of the earth will grow strangely dim, in the light of His glory and grace."

Being seated with Him in heavenly places gives you a different perspective on things. He has provided a secret place that you can run to; a place where you can remain stable and fixed under the shadow of Almighty God, whose power no foe can withstand (Psalm 91:1 AMP). It is an abiding place, not just a place we visit in prayer. It is the consciousness of God's presence in our lives that keeps us vitally united to the Vine every moment, every hour of the day.

By definition, revival is renewed attention to something ignored or forgotten; renewed interest in religion after decline; revived from languishing; restoration to consciousness of new life.

Just as in the smell of a turkey roasting in the oven or homemade soup cooking on the stove whets your appetite, tasting the goodness of the Lord, basking in His presence and smelling that sweet fragrance, whets your appetite for more of Him. Have you noticed that just the picture of food is enough to make you hungry? Read the book of Acts and see what revival is like. The boldness, the freedom and the joy the disciples experienced along with the wonderful success in seeing true conversion, signs, wonders, and miracles will whet your appetite for God to send the Holy Ghost with fire in this same hour.

I am a very visual person and I love pictures and paintings. One day as I was sitting in an office waiting for an appointment, I noticed a beautiful country scene done in watercolor pastels across the room on the wall. It was a painting of a brook running through the woods in spring with a deer bent in anticipation of the pure water. On the other side of the brook were blossoming fields of daisies and a family of rabbits. Having grown up in the countryside of New York, a scene like that was very common. Now, living in the city, it had been a while since I had such beautiful surroundings in which to meander. During my wait in the office, I had time to "step into" that picture in my mind and take a nice long walk.

That was in 1993. For weeks during that time I had been praying in the Spirit and with my understanding and I would hear myself say, "Pretty picture, Lord, it's a pretty picture," but I had no real understanding of the words I prayed until that day when I saw this watercolor. As I walked down the lane of the country scene in my imagination, I saw the deer run off and the rabbits hop away. I followed the path around the bend and saw more flowers blooming and berry bushes, ripe with wild blackberries. In my thoughts I said, "What a pretty picture!"

Suddenly I heard the Lord say, "Revival is a pretty picture. Step into the picture and take a walk around the bend of the river; you will see your family members drawing waters from the wells of salvation. Just a little further down the lane marriages are restored, and bodies are healed. There are miracles, signs and wonders. The river is flowing and everywhere it goes, it brings life!" What a beautiful picture of the days ahead for the church.

Right now, we have been seeing that picture of revival that is refreshing the church. It's wonderful and it's lovely to step into! The river is flowing and God's people are being refreshed. It's beginning to rain, and the river is rising. What we are seeing now is just the beginning.

We must continue to step deeper into the waters of revival. Once we get out deep enough so that the waters are over our heads, we will be out of our control and totally in God's control.

# CHAPTER THREE

# LOOKS LIKE RAIN TO ME!

*"And it shall come to pass in the last days, God declares, that I will pour out of My Spirit upon all mankind, and your sons and your daughters shall prophesy [telling forth the divine counsels] and your young men shall see visions (divinely granted appearances), and your old men shall dream [divinely suggested] dreams. Yes, and on My menservants also and on My maidservants in those days I will pour out of My Spirit, and they shall prophesy [telling forth the divine counsels and predicting future events pertaining especially to God's kingdom]."*

—Acts 2:17-18 AMP

Rain is rain. I'd recognize it anywhere. Look around you and you can see it's beginning to rain. This is that which was spoken of by the prophet Joel, so what do we do now?

Zechariah 10:1 says to pray for the rain in the time of the latter rain. In other words, when you see it begin to rain, pray for more rain! How will you know if it's the time for the latter rain? Just look around you! I've got news for you, rain in Boston looks just like rain in Texas! Sometimes it's heavier than others, but rain is still rain!

Well, the latter rain in Israel looks like the former rain, it's just heavier. The latter rain prepares the fields for harvest and comes to ripen up the fruit to get it ready for picking! If you want to know if what we are seeing around us today is this rain, go back to the book of Acts.

> *"But you shall receive power (ability, efficiency, and might) when the Holy Spirit has come upon you, and you shall be My witnesses in Jerusalem and all Judea and Samaria and to the ends (the very bounds) of the earth."*                          —Acts 1:8 AMP

> *"When suddenly there came a sound from heaven like the rushing of a violent tempest blast, and it filled the whole house in which they were sitting.*
> *And there appeared to them tongues resembling fire, which were separated and distributed and which settled on each one of them. And they were all filled (diffused throughout their souls) with the Holy Spirit and began to speak in other (different, foreign) languages (tongues), as the Spirit kept giving them clear and loud expression [in each tongue in appropriate words]."*          —Acts 2:2-4 AMP

Have you noticed a renewed fervor for tongues? Have you noticed anybody diffused with joy? Have you seen boldness, where folks just can't help but tell what God is doing? Have you seen your fellow believers stumbling out of services drunk in the Holy Ghost? Are you hearing sons and daughters prophesying? Have you noticed how many young men are being raised up with vision and life-long dreams of older men are being fulfilled? Rain is rain. Think it not strange! Christ's disciples are being rained upon in this hour. It's just like the former rain, only heavier. The former and latter rain together has come with a purpose to fill believers with the Holy Ghost and fire. It has come to make us a sign and a wonder and to ripen the fields for the greatest harvest ever.

Before He left for His heavenly home, Jesus told His disciples to wait for the Holy Spirit to come upon them. In Acts 1:8 He said, "You shall receive power (ability, efficiency, and might) when the Holy Spirit has come upon you." In Luke 24:49 He told them not to leave Jerusalem without it! They had no idea what they were waiting for, but they knew it was a prerequisite to leaving Jerusalem.

For three and a half years, Jesus had pumped the disciples full of Himself, the Word of God. Now, they needed something more before they went out to carry the good news into all the earth with signs and wonders following.

They waited in the upper room until suddenly the winds began to blow, the fire fell, and it settled on each one present. They were diffused throughout their being with joy unspeakable, full of glory. Suddenly they could express themselves only in tongues, a heavenly language recognized by many as dialects from various regions of the country.

Those who were once subdued and cautious about their connection to Jesus boldly proclaimed His power and might and they took it to the streets. Amidst mockery and scoffing, they continued to proclaim the good news with signs and wonders following. Overwhelmed by God's goodness and His mercy, they could not be contained in an upper room. They had to spread out and carry the good news everywhere. Day after day, with many coming and going, they continued to gather in the temple to praise, to pray, and to be filled again and again. Everyone had stories to tell of God's works to undo and destroy the works of the devil. Blind eyes were opening, the deaf were hearing, the lame walking, leaping and praising God.

They were so full of God that they were wall-to-wall Holy Ghost! When their eyes were fixed on the lame, they were raised to their feet. When their hands were laid upon the sick, they became the very hands of Christ extended, and power flowed through them to meet the need. When they spoke the word of deliverance to those that were bound, the captives broke free, never to be enslaved again! What a day! What an hour! And, it's raining again!

Some today, like the religious of that day, stand scoffing and mocking, saying, "Are these men and women drunk so early in the morning? Where do they get off being so bold?" They have been in the latter rain and are soaked and can't help but tell what God has done!

Paul prayed in Ephesians 3:19-21 that we would experience for ourselves the length, height, depth, and breadth of the love of God; that we would be filled through our whole being with the richest measure of His divine presence and be a body wholly filled and flooded with God Himself! He wants us to be absolutely saturated with His power, ability, efficiency and might, so that we too, can impact our world like the disciples turning it right side up (Acts 17:6)!

When you see the rain and hear it coming, don't open your umbrella and keep yourself from getting wet because we've been waiting for this rain! It's ripening the fields for harvest. For us as believers, it is softening the ground of our hearts, making us pliable and ready for the Master's good use. It is providing fresh water for us to drink, the living water that satisfies our thirsty souls. It is filling us with glory in preparation for us to spill that glory, so God can cover the whole earth with it.

Revival is on the calendar of God. He plans to visit every corner of the earth with a mighty outpouring of His Spirit that changes the course of events. It has already begun. It's the "new thing" of which Isaiah 43:19 speaks. Will you make room for it? Will you flow with it? Just get into the waters of refreshing and let them wash, cleanse, fill, and carry you!

Will you let God rid you of the hindrances in your own heart that make it difficult for you to completely give yourself over to Him? Revival brings change, first in our own hearts and lives. Soon those changes become obvious to others, and they too will be encouraged to open their hearts to the fresh touch of God.

In Galatians 3, Paul speaks of the work God has begun in us as believers. He questions the Galatians in verse 3, *"...having begun your new life spiritually with the Holy Spirit, are you now reaching perfection by dependence on the flesh?"* Surely we won't be so foolish as to think we will be able to become all that God wants us to be by our own power, but we will be persuaded as Philippians 1:6 declares that *"He Who began a good work in you will continue until the day of Jesus Christ [right up to the time of His return], developing [that good work] and perfecting and bringing it to full completion in you* (AMP)."

## CHAPTER 4

# WHAT'S THE PURPOSE?

*"For as the rain and snow come down from the heavens, and return not there again, but water the earth and make it bring forth and sprout...so shall My word be that goes forth from My mouth...it shall prosper in the thing for which I sent it."* —Isaiah 55:10-11 AMP

We probably all can't say we enjoy rainy days. They are perfect for reading a good book, or getting closets cleaned, but not always our favorite, especially if they show up in the middle of vacation... several of them in a row!

For a couple of years in the early 1990's, we scheduled our summers to travel through New England and up the East Coast Maritimes of Canada, preaching at churches along the way and camping with our sons. It was a little challenging to get dressed up for church services from the campgrounds. We drew a lot of stares at the camp showers, but we managed all right, except for those rainy days. There is only so much four people can do inside a camper! Night after night, we would go to churches and preach about the outpouring of God's Spirit and more rain would come! It was as if God was opening the windows of heaven and letting us see in the natural what we were experiencing in the Spirit. At one point, my husband forbade me to say even say the word "rain!" "Talk about the glory, or His presence," he'd say, *"but don't mention rain!"*

Years later as I was sitting in a hotel room watching the rain pour down outside, I was glad that I had nowhere to go outside of the hotel. I was only to speak downstairs in a ballroom later that day and wouldn't have to get out in the rain. The Lord began to speak to my heart and said, "You wouldn't really consider yourself a 'rainy day' person, would you?" I thought, "Not really. I enjoy a rainy day once in a while, especially if I can curl up with a good book and stay in bed!" Then I heard Him say, "Some people love rainy days, but even those who don't, enjoy the results!"

This prompted me to think of what rain produces. I thought about the flowers that would bloom profusely and the lush green grass. I thought about the tasty vegetables from the garden, and the lovely trees blossoming.

He interrupted my thoughts and said, "If people only knew what the rain would do for them, they would throw away their umbrellas and rush to get in it!"

When God pours out His Spirit and you experience the downpour, it can mess up your hair, your clothes can get a little disheveled, perhaps you've sweated through your clothes from dancing, or cried your makeup off from weeping in His presence. You may have been on the carpet several times, and are wrinkled, but on the inside the soaking has done you so much good. You may not even realize all the good it has done until you see how pliable your heart has become. All the hardness that was once there has now been softened by the rain and, like flowers blossoming, you have begun to break through. You're reaching up to God in a fresh way. You're bearing fruit and what is flowing out of your life is appealing to others.

When you read the book of Acts, you can see what the outpouring did for those who experienced it. They became different people. Just weeks before the outpouring of the Holy Spirit, some of these people denied even knowing Jesus, now they were boldly declaring their faith in Him. When threatened to stay quiet, they declared truth anyway. They were so filled they couldn't help but spill! Signs and wonders were everywhere. In Acts 3 when they turned to the lame man and offered him what they had, they simply said, "look on us." The man quickly fastened his eyes on them and he rose up walking, leaping and praising God! They sang, danced, and leaped. They were free! They had been filled to the brim with the power of the Holy Ghost and they were splashing it everywhere! The Amplified Bible says they were "diffused throughout their beings with joy." This joy became their strength in the days that were ahead of them as they faced great persecution for the Gospel's sake. Suddenly, life was what Jesus, before He was caught up in the clouds, had told the disciples it would become. They were to do those works that Jesus had told them to do, but they wouldn't be without opposition. As the disciples preached the Good News with signs and wonders following, they found themselves meeting resistance, but their strength came from joining together with other believers. They lifted their hands to heaven and praised God, being filled again with His power.

> *"And now, Lord observe their threats and grant to Your bondservants [full freedom] to declare Your message fearlessly, while You stretch out Your hand to cure and to perform signs and wonders through the authority and by the power of the name of Your holy Child and Servant, Jesus. And when they had prayed, the place in which they were assembled was shaken; and they were all filled with the Holy Spirit, and they continued to speak the Word of God with freedom and boldness and courage."* —Acts 4:29–31 AMP

# CHAPTER 5

# JOY MEANS STRENGTH

*"...do not be vague and thoughtless and foolish, but understanding and firmly grasping what the will of the Lord is. And do not get drunk with wine, but ever be filled and stimulated with the [Holy] Spirit."*
—Ephesians 5:17-18 AMP

Forty years had passed since Pentecost and revival was still sweeping the land. Conversions were at an all time high. There was no containing the church. You couldn't kill off a few and keep the good news quiet.

In Ephesians, Paul encouraged the disciples to stay vigilant. Remember guys, "don't be vague, thoughtless, or foolish, but understand and firmly grasp the will of God. Do not be drunk with wine but be ever-filled and stimulated with the power of the Holy Spirit, speaking to yourselves and to one another with psalms, hymns and spiritual songs, making melody in your hearts unto the Lord" (Ephesians 5:17-19). Paul is assuring the believers that they need not run low on God's power, but can keep themselves running on a full tank by speaking and praising! They could keep primed the pump of the well of salvation that God gave to each of us. Isaiah 12:3 says, "with joy we draw waters out of our well of salvation." Each of us has a well. Even when there isn't a camp meeting to attend or a prophet in town, you can go to your own well, and drink in the refreshing waters!

You may have always used a bucket to draw water at a well, but God's Word says to draw out refreshing with joy! You may say, "That's my problem. I have no joy." Oh, yes you do! Joy is not having everything going your way, but the fruit of God's Holy Spirit in your life. You may have to "count it all joy in the midst of various trials and temptations" (James 1:2). Just begin rehearsing God's faithfulness and remind yourself that you have a God who never leaves nor forsakes you. You are not alone. Remind yourself that He makes a way when there doesn't seem to be one and works all things together for good. He's on your side, so who can be against you (Psalm 27:1)? As you remind yourself of these things, you can throw your head back and laugh because it's not over yet. God is working His plan for you to give you a hope in the final outcome (Jeremiah 29:11). Before you know it, there will be joy like a cool drink of water, refreshing your soul. His joy will be your strength. God has used joy time and again to bring strength to His people. Remember when Abraham laughed the laugh of faith? God had just promised him he would have a son at 100 years of age (Genesis 17)! How about Nehemiah 8:10, when the Word of the Lord came to the children of Israel after they had spent seventy years in captivity, "Weep no more, the joy of the Lord shall be your strength?"

For some, it seems that this joyful, exuberant move of God is unnecessary. They argue that these are sober times and don't believe that God can be in such frivolity. Without understanding the purpose, they find this more difficult to embrace. However, the Scriptures are very clear that the purpose of joy is strength!

Speaking of the deliverance of the children of Israel following seventy years of captivity, Psalm 126:1 says they were as those that dreamed. Mouths were filled with laughter and their voices with singing. Can you imagine, overnight, becoming so free and so full of joy you thought you were dreaming? I can, because that's just how it happened for me! One day I was weighed down with cares and anxieties, struggling to cast them on the Lord. My body was tormented and in pain from ulcers. I couldn't enjoy eating the spicy foods that I loved because of the repercussions. Everyone's needs seemed like a demand on me personally. I was short-tempered and irritable. Suddenly, the Word of the Lord came to me with a big dose of the Holy Ghost and fell upon me, knocking me off of my feet. I felt the joy that rippled through my belly was like a river of living water. It carried the care and worry away cleansing and soothing my insides, healing me of ulcers. It lifted the burdens off of my shoulders, as the anointing destroyed the yoke (Isaiah 10:27).

I woke up the next morning with a song on my lips and laughter in my heart because I was free! I thought that surely I must have been dreaming. Many years have gone by since and I do my best to drink waters from my well of salvation continually, staying ever-filled and stimulated with the power of the Holy Spirit, speaking to myself in psalms, hymns and spiritual songs, making melody in my heart to the Lord (Ephesians 5:17-19).

God wants us strong to do exploits for Him. His joy is to be our strength, restoring us with passion for the lost.

> *"Restore to me the joy of Your salvation and uphold me with a willing spirit. Then will I teach transgressors Your ways, and sinners shall be converted and return to You."* —Psalm 51:12-13 AMP

In the introduction to Philippians in THE MESSAGE BIBLE, Eugene Peterson wrote...

"This is Paul's happiest letter, and the happiness is infectious...Happiness is not a word we can understand by looking it up in the dictionary...something more like apprenticeship is required, being around someone who out of years of devoted discipline shows us, by his or her entire behavior, what it is...an apprentice mostly acquires skill by daily and intimate association with a "master"...Paul doesn't tell us we can be happy or how to be happy. He simply and unmistakably IS happy. None of his circumstances contribute to his joy. He wrote from a jail cell, his work was under attack by competitors, and after twenty years or so of hard traveling in the service of Jesus, he was tired...but circumstances are incidental compared to the life of Jesus, the Messiah that Paul experiences from the inside. For it is a life that not only happened at a certain point in history, but continues to happen, spilling out into the lives of those who receive him...Christ is among much else, the revelation that God cannot be contained or hoarded. It is this "spilling out" quality of Christ's life that accounts for the happiness of Christians, for joy is life in excess, the overflow of what cannot be contained within any one person."

## CHAPTER SIX

# LIVING IN THE RIVER
# OF GOD'S GLORY

Personal Testimony by
Vicki Jamison-Peterson

As many experiences as I have had over the years as a minister, never has anything made an impact upon me to the extent that the manifestation of God's glory and joy did. Now, as people came to my services, they would become what we call "drunk in the Spirit" like in Acts, chapter 2. I would lay hands on people and the glory of God would manifest through joy and laughter, and the services would go into extended revivals. It seemed to be a turn in my ministry from the healing anointing, but I knew it was God.

For me personally, it seemed to open the door to witness to people who were drawn to me. It was a very different experience in my life, because while I love witnessing to people, never had I experienced just being like a flame and people like moths being drawn to me.

On one occasion, sitting alone in Chicago's O'Hare Airport during a winter blizzard, I had not expected to strike up a conversation. So, when a gentleman rolled a woman in a wheelchair a few feet in front of me, I glanced at her briefly, then resumed reading my magazine. I was totally absorbed in the news.

Since I was the only other person there, the woman struck up a conversation with me. "This is going to be my last trip," she said. Somewhat distracted, I said, "Really?" I quickly became aware of God's presence and immediately moved into the seat next to her so I could touch her. I put my arm around her and let her tell me about her condition.

The woman suffered from critical arthritis. I found out the doctor had told her if she wanted to see her family again, she'd better do it right away because she would never travel again.

As she recounted her story, I just listened and held my arm around her, quietly allowing the anointing of God to flow into her body. I learned that she was a Christian, but she didn't know God still heals today. So I shared some Scriptures with her about healing, explaining that it was God's will to heal those who are ill.

"I didn't know that!" she exclaimed.

Within a matter of a minute or two, I asked her, "Why don't you move your legs now?" She had already told me that she couldn't move her legs at all. However, I knew that the anointing of God's power to heal was present. The moment the woman tried to move her legs, she screamed in shock, "Oh! I can move my legs!" God had instantaneously and totally healed her! Within ten minutes of sitting in a deserted part of O'Hare Airport, the woman who rolled up in a wheelchair walked out praising God! Her life was completely transformed that day by the glory of God!

If we are going to stay full of joy, we have to stay in the river of God's glory. Scripture says "A merry heart does good, like medicine" (Proverbs 17:22 NKJV). Today, research is revealing that a merry heart really does do good, particularly to the immune system in increasing antibody-producing cells and activating virus-fighting T cells. It also has positive effects upon the brain.

Karen S. Peterson, quoted in *USA Today* with her comments reprinted in the *Tulsa World,* says, "A good belly laugh boosts the body's immune system and reduces hormones that cause stress. A positive state of mind helps keep healthy people well and helps the sick recover."[1] In this same article, Peterson stated that even smiling releases endorphins — brain chemicals that make you feel good.

Again, Peterson writes, "In his review of the research, Montclair, New Jersey, psychologist Paul McGhee notes that frequent laughter relaxes muscles, helps control pain, may lower blood pressure, and helps manage stress while increasing joy."

She also indicates that natural killer cells that attack tumor cells and viruses, without the help of other cells, increase their activity with laughter. An article in the Orlando Sentinel, "Research Confirms! Laughter is Best Medicine," lists a few "Facts About Laughter." Here are some of these facts:

*Laughing is aerobic, providing a workout for the diaphragm and increasing the body's ability to utilize oxygen.

*Laughter increases immunity to infections by instantly increasing a flood of disease-fighting cells and proteins into the blood.

*Brain wave activity changes when we catch the punch line of a joke.[2]

This same article states, "Stress hormones also...increase the number of sticky cells called platelets that can cause fatal obstructions in arteries."

Peterson reports that two Loma Linda University professors, Dr. Lee Berk and Dr. Stanley Tan, have shown in their studies that "laughing lowers blood pressure, increases muscle flexion, and triggers a flood of beta endorphins, the brain's natural morphine-like compounds that can induce a sense of euphoria...Health dividends are multiplied for those who indulge regularly in big ol' belly laughs ... Laughter is inexpensive and it has no negative side effects!"

We are carriers of God's presence to the world! God desires to use each of us in unusual ways, in unusual places – not just in a church setting. He wants His glory in all the earth. Our God is not One to be contained.

In his 1828 *American Dictionary of the English Language,* Noah Webster defines "glory" as brightness, luster, splendor, magnificence ... In Scripture, the divine presence ... as the magnificence of it; to exult with joy; to rejoice.

In II Corinthians 3:18, the Apostle Paul states, *"But we all, with open face beholding as in a glass the glory of the Lord, are changed into the same image from glory to glory, even as by the Spirit of the Lord* (KJV)*."*

God's glory—His splendor, His honor, and His prevailing power—comes to change us, to make us like Him. In that process of changing from one degree of glory to another, God multiplies or increases the presence of His glory within us. As a result, His glory becomes so great in our lives that even before we have said anything to people about Jesus, people can sense His presence when they are in our presence. He overwhelms us with Himself.

God desires that we carry His presence to the world. As we simply yield or respond to Him, He will release His glory through us to those around us. Often, I'll go up to a salesperson and ask, "How are you doing today?" If they say, " Oh, I'm sick," many times I'll take their hand and answer, "Well, in the Name of Jesus...Now, how do you feel?" With a startled expression, the individual will look amazed, then sputter, "Fine!"

It's not at all complicated to share God's glory. As Christians —as "Christ-in-us-ones"—we are anointed to take His Name and carry His glory to the world. This isn't solely the responsibility of those who stand in the five-fold ministry office. It is the number one ministry of every believer. We are all called to carry the glory and transforming presence of our God into the world. But before we can carry Him to the world, we must allow Him to overflow in us.

That overflow comes as we open a path for the glory of God. But, you may say, "I've already given an opening to God." I assure you, He is waiting for you to open up more. The degree to which you allow the glory to overflow in you is the degree to which the glory can flow through you.

It is thrilling to feel God's presence inside you so strongly that you laugh or weep because when He comes in, you change! At times my behavior seemed excessive to some. And it was – excessively joyful! The "joy" movement, as some refer to it, was a time of experiencing a profound connection with God's nature and His presence. His presence is always needed – this was not just a phase. The important thing is not whether you laugh, fall, roll, or run. The important thing is that you choose to respond to the Holy Spirit. Because when you respond to Him, you make a pathway for the glory of God to enter in and saturate you. What is happening is God is creating in us a hunger for Him. And because we're hungry for God, we're open to whatever He wants to do.

God inspires us to pursue Him that He may lay hold of us. In gradual stages, He stirs us to open our hearts to Him. Why? He's setting us up. Step by step, every time we respond to His presence, God draws us a little closer to Himself. He is guiding us into direct encounters with His manifest presence that will change us forever. (It's not a one-time encounter.) The purpose? To get us in position for His grand finale—the greatest outpouring of glory the earth has ever known!

Just as we have learned to confess who we are in Christ and to fill our hearts with His Word, we must also learn to yield to the Holy Spirit, for He is the One Who activates the power of the Word in our lives.

In this hour, like never before, the Spirit of God will release mighty demonstrations of the Word in the earth by the power of His glory. That glory will flow through us, the Body of Christ, to a world without Him – a world looking for a God Whose presence is real. All we stand in need of – spirit, soul, and body – is found in the glory. Recognize it. Yield to it. Receive it. Then, when God wants to display a tangible demonstration of His Spirit and power to the world, He will do it through you and me. We are temples of the living God, containers of His presence, and carriers of His joy and glory!

CHAPTER SEVEN

# AHHH—I COULD HAVE HAD A V-8!

We make choices everyday to live our lives happy or sad, frustrated or at peace. Sometimes I could just kick myself for being all upset, and worrying about the outcome of things, especially when I see God's faithfulness demonstrated again and again. I think to myself....ahhh, I could have had a V-8! I could have relaxed and enjoyed the journey, but instead I pressed on in my own strength, trying to figure out what to do, and in the meantime missed wonderful opportunities to be a witness for Christ!

THE MESSAGE BIBLE hits the nail on the head in Psalm 73:16-17 where it says...."when I tried to figure it all out, all I got was a splitting headache! Until I entered the sanctuary of God, then I saw the whole picture." Jehovah-Jireh, the God who has already seen the need and made the provision is waiting to show Himself strong on our behalf. No wonder He who sits in the heavens laughs (Psalm 2:4). He sees the end of the wicked! He knows the end of the story, and if we'll read His book, we'll realize there is a happy ending for us too!

*"I know the thoughts and plans I have for you,
says the Lord, thoughts and plans for welfare and
peace and not for evil, to give you hope in your
final outcome."*                    —Jeremiah 29:11 AMP

When Christ left this earth, He endowed us with the
greatest gift—

"Peace, I leave with you; My own peace I now give
and bequeath to you. Not as the world gives, do I give to
you. Do not let your hearts be troubled, neither let it be
afraid. [Stop allowing yourselves to be agitated and dis-
turbed and do not permit yourselves to be fearful and
intimidated, cowardly and unsettled] John 14:27 (AMP)."

All of that agitation, disturbedness, fear and intimidation
sure does rob you of joy! In John l6:33, Jesus admitted to
His disciples that in the world they'd have tribulation, trials,
distress and frustration. He told them to be of good cheer for
He had overcome the world. CHEER UP! God has made a
way, even when there seems to be no way, and He'll bring
you through every time. If we'll cast our cares over on the
Lord, as He instructed us, we can actually enjoy life while
God handles our problems!

*"He (God) will rescue you in six troubles; in seven
nothing that is evil [for you] will touch you. In famine
He will redeem you from death, and in war from the
power of the sword. You shall be hidden from the
scourge of the tongue, neither shall you be afraid of
destruction when if comes....at destruction and
famine you shall laugh..."*          —Job 5:19-22 AMP

It's hard to laugh when nothing is very funny but
James challenges us in chapter one, verse two to "consider it wholly joyful, whenever you are enveloped in or

encounter trials of any sort or fall into various temptations." I have a friend who taught on this passage of Scripture in power and demonstration! She said that to count it all joy, literally means to throw a party, so when she and her family faced challenges they would celebrate, cake, noisemakers and all!

Proverbs 17:22 says "laughter (or a happy heart) is good medicine" and again in Proverbs 15:15 we read, "...he who has a glad heart has a continual feast [regardless of circumstances] (AMP)." This joy not only keeps us full of God, but will keep us healthy as well. Our part is to tap into the supply of joy available to us.

I remember one time living in Boston, when I received a report that my mom was very ill in upstate New York. I packed my car and filled my tank with gas so I could leave early in the morning to drive the ten hours between us. I put the pedal to the metal and drove hard, stopping only long enough to use a restroom, and stayed focused on getting there as quickly as possible.

I know this will sound really "blonde," but after nine hours my car started acting up and I laid hands on the dashboard, commanding it to run as it was created to, when suddenly I got one more thrust from the engine, and it sputtered to a stop as I pulled over to the side of the highway. Then it hit me! I had been driving for nine hours, and had never stopped to refuel! I was too busy thinking, and praying and trying to figure out what I'd do when I got to my mother, and on and on....I never even thought to stop for gas!

Do you have any idea how many gas stations I passed by on the Massachusetts turnpike, and New York thruway traveling that day? No less than fifty, to be sure.

Right there, on the side of the road, the Spirit of God began to speak to me..."You can't continue to live your life on an empty tank either. You must take time to refuel. Don't pass by those spiritual fueling stations I've provided for you—church on Sunday, special prayer on Tuesday, fellowship with believers on Wednesday, and time in My presence every day for it is what keeps you filled with My power, and grace to run your race, and do it with JOY!"

CHAPTER EIGHT

# LET THE RIVER FLOW

*"There is a river whose streams shall make glad the city of God..."* —Psalm 46:4 AMP

As mentioned before, our family frequently camped summers in New England. One of the first summers we traveled, we had bought a used, pop-up camper and were looking forward to visiting the churches of New England and enjoying family time together camping. We had picked a campground that advertised river tubing and hurried to set up camp on arrival to have time to go tubing before the sun set. We all ran to the river and were disappointed to find the waters low and rather than a rushing river, we found nothing more than a babbling brook. Determined to go tubing, our sons got in the river and maneuvered their tubes through the rocks to catch what current there was and enjoy the ride. They urged Steve and myself to come along, but the extra weight we put on the tubes seemed to dispel any current in the river. The ride we had was a painful one over the rocks and debris.

We went to bed that night in our camper hearing predictions of thundershowers and joked that we'd find out if our used camper had any leaks. Well, it did and we got soaked in the night, but the good news was the rain had caused the river to rise by morning. It had become more than a babbling brook, but now rushing rapids and our tubes flew down the river.

Just as the thundershowers raised the river, the rain of the Holy Spirit is causing the spiritual waters to rise and what was once a struggle is getting easier as we are able to move into deeper waters.

In Ezekiel 47, we get the picture that Ezekiel had as the spiritual guide led him into deeper waters.

> *"And when the man went on eastward with the measuring line in his hand, he measured a thousand cubits, and he caused me to pass through the waters, waters that were ankle-deep. Again he measured a thousand cubits and caused me to pass through the waters, waters that reached to the knees. Again he measured a thousand cubits and caused me to pass through the waters, waters that reached to the loins. Afterward he measured a thousand, and it was a river that I could not pass through, for the waters had risen, waters to swim in, a river that could not be passed over or through."* —Ezekiel 47:3-5 AMP

God is calling us into the deep where the waters are over our head. He wants us to stop trying to figure everything out. He wants us to stop operating out of our own strength. Instead, He wants His waters to carry us.

If you read further in Ezekiel, you will see that the waters flowed out of the sanctuary into the Dead Sea. When the waters touched every dead thing, they began to produce life.

If we live like we are supposed to live, pouring out God's love, His saving and healing power on to a thirsty world, it is inevitable that we will need to be filled over and over again. Understand the principle of Luke 6:38, and know that as you give, it will be given to you. What will be given to you? Whatever you gave! It works in every currency of exchange—love, kindness, time, money, hospitality, and grace. Just remember, it will also work as Luke 6 says, in reaping judgment and criticism.

Quit judging those around you who are filled with joy and boldly preaching Jesus. You will wind up filled with criticism and being judgmental and opinionated. Get in the river of God's blessings. Go with the flow and get saturated with God's love and presence. It will change your life!

Ezekiel 47:12 is a powerful promise for people that will plant themselves along the river that flows from the sanctuary. There comes a time when you have tried all the churches in town. It's time to get planted. Put your roots down deep. Start thriving and flourish like a cedar of Lebanon (Psalm 92:12). I believe that if you will, you will get in on this supernatural fruitbearing.

> *"And on the banks of the river on both its sides, there shall grow all kinds of trees for food; their leaf shall not fade nor shall their fruit fail [to meet the demand]. Each tree shall bring forth new fruit every month, [these supernatural qualities being] because their waters came from out of the sanctuary. And their fruit shall be for food and their leaves for healing."*
> —Ezekiel 47:12 AMP

Believers have always been compared to trees (See Psalm 1, Jeremiah 17, and Psalm 92). If you get planted along the banks of this river of revival, you will begin to see some supernatural things happen. God is making us all carriers of His glory. Our leaves will be for healing, the fruit we bear shall not fail to meet the demand with new fruit every month! People will say that this is supernatural. They will come and pick our fruit and the fruit they pick will be ripe and tasty! Some of you have been complaining because people are picking on you, but that's what the fruit in your life is there for, to be picked!

These days will be days of such rejoicing as we see answers to prayer after prayer as the fruit born from abiding in the Vine is being picked and eaten to satisfy the needs of people. We will surely say as John 15 does, "Apart from You, I can do nothing. But, vitally united to the Vine, we will bear much fruit and our fruit shall remain!"

CHAPTER NINE

# CONTAINERS OF THE GLORY

*"Whoever cleanses himself, [from what is ignoble and unclean who separates himself from contact with contaminating and corrupting influences] will then be a vessel set apart and useful for honorable and notable purposes, consecrated and profitable to the Master, fit and ready for any good work."*
—II Timothy 2:21 AMP

It's amazing that when I travel and arrive home in the evening, or even when I'm at the office and come home late in the day, I really don't notice the dust in my house. When I happen to stay at home for a day and the sun is shining in brightly, my goodness! I don't realize how much dust accumulates!

This is a good comparison to those times when we come to linger in God's presence. In the light of His glory, our "dust" shows up, most of which has accumulated over a period of time. We've been so busy, we really didn't notice, but then we are faced with a choice. Will we submit ourselves to the work of the Holy Spirit to change us, or do we quickly get busy again to avoid coming into the light where it all showed up in the first place?

I know that the Lord is changing me from one degree of glory to another, but sometimes I just want to get it all over with at once. You probably feel like that sometimes, too. There are times that we, like Paul on the road to Damascus, are confronted with the light of God's glory and it illuminates our shortcomings. Challenged with that light, we are faced with choices. We can allow God to arrest us and convert us, or we can try to escape His hold.

In the light of God's glory, decisions must be made. Will we come clean, or continue to cover in darkness our companionship with the world?

> *"You groped your way through that murk once, but no longer. You're out in the open now. The bright light of Christ makes your way plain. So no more stumbling around. Get on with it! The good, the right, the true—these are the actions appropriate for daylight hours. Figure out what will please Christ, and then do it."*
> —Ephesians 5:8-10 The Message Bible

We need not fear or despise this chastening of the Lord. He loves us and wants to shine through us. The purer we become, the purer will be the flow of God through us. We've all heard the expression "many are called, but few are chosen." I am told the original Hebrew says, "few chose."

II Timothy 2:21 says that if any man (or woman) desires to be a vessel of gold unto honor, he (or she) must keep themselves cleansed and uncontaminated from this world that they may be vessels of honor, fit and ready for the Master's good use. We can't excuse it. It is not up to God whether we are for ignoble or noble use. It is our choice. Many times we cry out, "God, use me!" But, we have a part to play.

If we really want to shine for Jesus, we're going to have to be run through the wash cycle, rinse cycle, maybe even some spot remover so that we can be as clean and transparent as possible.

> *"And be constantly renewed in the spirit of your mind [having a fresh mental and spiritual attitude], And put on the new nature (the regenerate self) created in God's image, [Godlike] in true righteousness and holiness."*     —Ephesians 4:23-24 AMP

> *"So that He might sanctify her, having cleansed her by the washing of water with the Word, That He might present the church to Himself in glorious splendor, without spot or wrinkle or any such things [that she might be holy and faultless]."* —Ephesians 5:26-27 AMP

It seems it would be so much easier if we could just throw our minds into a double-duty cycle on a Maytag washer in order to renew our mind, but God's word will do the job.

Please realize all this growth and change will not be done in your own strength. Galatians 5:22 says that bearing fruit is a work which His presence within us accomplishes.

You can come into the presence of the Lord, singing, worshiping, praying and sensing His presence, and yet hurry right back out of that presence, or, you can linger and allow it to become a part of you. When you make the decision not just to get into God's presence, but to let His presence get in you, it will continue to work in you even as you leave that church service, that godly conversation, or that time of fellowship in God's Word where He was so tangibly present and speaking to your heart. Don't just let the presence of God come on you. Let it abide in you to do a thorough work so that you will be prepared to pour out God's glory. He is asking you to be a vessel if you are willing to empty yourself of "self." He will provide the contents, and fill you with the fullness of Himself.

> *"And all of us, as with unveiled face, [because we] continued to behold [in the Word of God] as in a mirror the glory of the Lord, are constantly being transfigured into His very own image in ever increasing splendor and from one degree of glory to another; [for this comes] from the Lord [Who is] the Spirit."*
> —II Corinthians 3:18 AMP

Change! We will be doing it until Jesus returns or we cross over to the other side. Until then, it is one degree of glory to another. God is committed to your transformation, this metamorphosis of your whole being until you are conformed into the image of Christ and share His likeness. Philippians 1:6 (KJV) says, "...He which hath begun a good work in you will perform it until the day of Jesus Christ."

Proverbs says that we must not be like a horse or mule, who has to be bridled and yanked this way or that, but learn to yield to the Greater One. Let Him guide you and clean you out! Remember, the same water that refreshes, also cleanses. He wants to do a new thing in you, but will you make room for it?

On the day of Pentecost they were baptized with the Holy Ghost and fire. Somehow today we manage to get the Holy Ghost and avoid the fire. We need to ask God to baptize us anew with the Holy Ghost along with the fire so that it can burn out of us every sin and hindrance, burning into us a passion to abandon our lives to the call and destiny of God. IT'S A NEW DAY! The Holy Spirit is being poured out with fire and it is up to us to allow the total cleansing and purging of our hearts and to welcome this work within.

You may be going places and doing things for God already. God may be using you. You don't see why you need this work done in you. John 15 speaks of a pruning process. Pruning is a "cutting back of something" with one purpose, to allow you to blossom again with a greater fullness and greater fruit bearing capacity. Even mature trees need to be maintained by the pruning process, which allows them to continue to bear fruit in their old age. As we abide in God's Word, John 15 says we are cleansed and pruned by that Word, revealing anything in our lives that hinders us, and cutting it off.

# CHAPTER TEN

# THE EBB AND FLOW OF THE RIVER

*"Incline your ear [submit and consent to the divine will] and come to Me; hear and your soul will revive..."*
—Isaiah 55:3 AMP

It was the summer or '93 and our family went camping on Prince Edward Island in Canada. I was sitting by the ocean on a nearly secluded beach. It was the first time we had scheduled a real vacation, no ministry engagements or social commitments, just ten days to be with the kids. Our cell phones wouldn't work in that remote spot and I secretly cheered to think that no one would be calling. We had told the children (then four and twelve) that we were going to have morning devotions on the beach to pray, share Bible truths, and to just talk. That particular morning they weren't so restless, because the tide was out and the lure of the waves to come play didn't distract them. I stared out over the water just overwhelmed at God's goodness to give us this time and I watched as the tide drew further and further out. The Holy Spirit was ministering to my heart. "The tide is out. Enjoy the peace and quiet. There is an ebb and flow you must learn. The earth is Mine and I have established it upon the currents and the rivers (Psalm 24:2). Your life is like the ocean. It has an ebb and flow. There is a time for everything; times where everything is moving very rapidly and times where things get very still. Learn to replenish in those quiet times, not fill your schedule when I give you times of refreshing. Learn to recognize when the tide is out, and draw near to Me. Get quiet and listen...that your soul may revive" (Isaiah 55:3).

He had spoken to me that the tide would turn again and just as He said, the waters soon began to lap against the shore. We had to move the beach blanket and the children began running in and out of the waves.

You've heard it prophesied. You can smell the salt in the air. The tide is coming in again. It's lapping against the shore; another wave, another move, the greater harvest.

"All this filling has purpose. This wave will not be as before, for the former wave has knocked you off your feet. Rather, this wave will put you on your feet to carry the power of the Gospel to the uttermost parts of the earth with signs, wonders, and miracles accompanying you. It will give you power to do what you could never do. It is by My grace and by My power that you will be thrust into the field to reap a harvest in this hour. So continue in My presence. Continue to be renewed, for it is not just about you, but those whom you will touch with your outstretched hands. You have been filled to spill My glory throughout every land."[3]

# CHAPTER ELEVEN

# MY CUP RUNNETH OVER

*"The Lord is my Shepherd...He leads me beside the still and restful waters. He refreshes and restores my life...You anoint my head with oil; my [brimming] cup runs over."*

—Psalm 23:1-3, 5 AMP

I made the mistake years ago of assuming that the river of revival was just one big rapid. No river is entirely a rapid! Somewhere along the river, it will take a turn. For a season it will become seemingly still, lacking a current, but the waters are always moving. The rapids are a thrill, but there's a lot to be said for the quiet, placid waters. Catch your breath, lie back in the sun and notice what's around you.

Life can appear to be like rapids. God is moving and it is glorious, but anyone that has lived very long knows that constant movement is exhausting. Our souls require replenishment that goes beyond a good night's sleep. That may do it for your body, but not for your inner man. Psalm 42:1 (NKJV) says, "As the deer pants for the water brooks, so pants my soul [my inner self] for You, O God."

I once was told a story of American missionaries on a journey through the jungles of Africa to set up a mission outpost. They had engaged natives to take them on their journey and haul their trunks of belongings through the jungle. After several days of the missionaries driving the natives to make time and arrive as quickly as possible, the natives simply sat in their tracks refusing to go on. When they communicated with their interpreter as to what the problem was, he simply answered, "They say you have moved them too quickly and that they must take time for their souls to catch up with them."

We must realize that in the rivers of revival, the same waters that carry us, also cleanse us and refresh us. As there is a rhythm to the waters, there must be a rhythm to our lives.

> "God—You're my God! I can't get enough of You! I've worked up such hunger and thirst for God, traveling across dry and weary deserts. So here I am in the place of worship, eyes open, drinking in Your strength and glory. In Your generous love I am really living at last!"    —Psalm 63:1 THE MESSAGE BIBLE

Just like our bodies need replenishment with pure, clean water, our souls are also thirsty to be replenished. The experts say that by the time you "feel" thirsty, you are already dehydrated. Dehydration leaves you listless, confused and weary, and can even damage your internal organs. Our bodies are actually made up of eighty percent water; that's why we are told to replenish ourselves with at least six to eight glasses of water every day! We must not allow ourselves to get dehydrated in our spirits! Waiting on the Lord will renew your strength. A divine exchange is made in His presence that allows you to "mount up with wings like eagles, run and not grow weary, walk and not faint" (Isaiah 40:31).

I have done a lot of running around in my life, but to run and not get weary is another story, but even more significant is the promise to walk and not faint! The consistency to make spiritual progress on a daily basis is dependent on the rhythm of your life in relationship to God.

> *"...Each of us is now a part of His resurrection body, refreshed and sustained at one fountain—His Spirit— where we all come to drink."*
> —I Corinthians 12:13 THE MESSAGE BIBLE

> *"...Your strength will come from settling down in complete dependence on Me..."*
> —Isaiah 30:15 THE MESSAGE BIBLE

In every race, there is a starting line where all runners begin and then end at a designated finish line. The whistle, gun shot, or flag releases everyone to run, but if you "jump the gun" at the starting line, you will be disqualified at the finish line, even though you may have run all five miles. Wait on God. He will give you a clear signal when He wants you to run.

Every morning we rise to run the race. We all have new mercies to start our day on equal footing. Some people rise just in time to run, but others are up earlier, stretching, preparing to run.

> *"God, the one and only—I'll wait as long as He says. Everything I need comes from Him, so why not? He's solid rock under my feet, breathing room for my soul, An impregnable castle: I'm set for life."*
> —Psalm 62:1-2 THE MESSAGE BIBLE

*"Guide me in Your truth and faithfulness and teach me, for You are the God of my salvation; for You [You only and altogether] do I wait [expectantly] all the day long."*
                                                —Psalm 25:5 AMP

There's nothing that prepares us more for each day than rising and communing with God. Andrew Murray has said that any soldier on the field who is out of ammunition and supplies knows he must lay low and radio for more supplies, yet believers rise every morning and head right into battle with no ammunition and no supply and wonder why they are weary and wounded before the day ends.

*"But those who wait for the Lord [who expect, look for, and hope in Him] shall change and renew their strength and power; they shall lift their wings and mount up [close to God] as eagles [mount up to the sun]; they shall run and not be weary, they shall walk and not faint or become tired."*    —Isaiah 40:31 AMP

A few years ago I had the opportunity to visit Israel. I'd always been told that the Word of God would come alive as I walked where Jesus had walked and it was true. I saw things and experienced things that made the simplest of Jesus' illustrations come alive. I also experienced the culture of the Jewish people and saw that by observing God's laws of Sabbath, they had established a rhythm to their week that replenished and restored them: body, soul and spirit. They took time to "fill".

Psalm 23 has come alive to me, as I have established my own Sabbath rest. Thank God that we no longer have to wait until Friday, because Jesus has become our Sabbath and He has rest waiting for those who believe. We read in Hebrews 4:10 that there remains a rest for the people of God who will cease from the strivings of their own human flesh and learn from Him. Don't miss verse 12, "for the Word of God is alive and full of power." You can rest when you put God's Word to work, sending it forth out of your mouth to heal and deliver from every pit of destruction (Psalm 107:20). When you are filled with God's Word, you can become alive, active, and full of power and be sent forth as a vessel to pour out the refreshing of the life of God to a lost and dying world.

God is not pouring out His Spirit in these days without purpose. Luke 4:18 says, "The Spirit of the Lord is upon Me, because he hath anointed Me..." Just as Jesus was anointed "because," we too are filled with purpose! We are to preach good news to the poor, announce release to the captives and recovery of sight to the blind, to send forth delivered those who are oppressed, downtrodden, bruised, crushed, and broken down by calamity.

He leads us beside those still waters, restores our souls, replenishing us so that we may be as an artesian well, bringing refreshing to others.

Years ago missionaries to Haiti built and opened an orphanage on some undeveloped land. They had been directed by the Lord to dig a well in a particular spot, but after days of drills digging, they hit only rock. The workers suggested that they try elsewhere, but the missionaries felt certain that they were in the spot the Lord had designated. The only solution was to send back to the States for bigger bits. Weeks later, as they resumed the project, those bigger bits pounded through the rock and suddenly a gusher thirty-five feet high shot up from the earth. The people danced and shouted and they soon realized that they hit an artesian well! By definition, an artesian well is an endless supply of spring water that runs beneath the impenetrable rock strata of the earth. Once they hit that water, they not only had the supply to meet their need for the orphanage, but they became the water supply for the entire community!

> *"Anyone who drinks the water I give will never thirst—not ever. The water I give will be an artesian spring within, gushing fountains of endless life."*
> —John 4:14 THE MESSAGE BIBLE

> *"On the final and climactic day of the Feast, Jesus took his stand. He cried out, 'If anyone thirsts, let him come to Me and drink. Rivers of living water will brim and spill out of the depths of anyone who believes in Me this way, just as the Scripture says.'"*
> —John 7:37-38 THE MESSAGE BIBLE

Jesus had been with the people for several days, eating and drinking "in the days of the great feast." Still full from dinner, He turned to these men and asked a ridiculous question, "Are you hungry and thirsty?" By now they had every opportunity to be satisfied filling up with fresh bread, fruits, meats, and the best wine. But, He was asking them, "Are you hungry for more?" Is there a longing on the inside of you for something that taking in more can't satisfy? He who hungers and thirsts for righteousness will be filled and out of his belly will flow rivers of living water. It's one thing to have a well of salvation of which Isaiah 12:3 speaks, where you can draw and satisfy your own thirst, but it is quite another thing to have a river flowing out to others. A river cannot be contained. It must flow and that is exactly what God wants you to do, flow! Let the life of God in you move out to others.

Share your peace, your joy, and your confidence in the Savior, Healer, Deliverer, and Lover of your soul. Share the hope that lies within. Don't bottle up your river. Release it to a lost, dying and thirsty world. The satisfaction won't come from just what you take in anymore; it will come from what flows out!

Have you ever thought about the numerous parts of God's Word referring to excess? At first glance, it would make God seem wasteful to cause cups to run over and open windows from heaven to pour out blessings without room enough to receive them. It is a waste if you miss the purpose of God's excess. By His very name, which reveals His nature, He is a God of MORE than enough. What do you suppose He wants done with the excess? It's easy to see that He has more in mind for us when He fills the cup, opens the window, feeds five thousand and still has baskets full of leftovers. He expects us, as His representatives on the earth, to be as generous with others as He has been to us, so that those who don't know Him can see who He really is through us.

According to II Corinthians 4:6-7, we carry in these frail human vessels the divine light of the Gospel. It's time to shine as bright lights in a dark and perverse world (Philippians 2:15).

Paul prayed in Ephesians 3:19 that we be "filled throughout our being with the richest measure of God's divine presence and be a body wholly filled and flooded with God Himself." Not just enough, but flooded to the more than enough stage! When you have been refreshed in God's presence, you can go out with a "cup that runneth over" (Psalm 23:5) and effortlessly spill life to all those around you. As long as you live life with just enough provision to meet your needs and just enough joy to make it through your day, and just enough peace to keep your mind at rest, you will miss out on God's highest and best. He makes your cup to run over so you can help meet the needs of others, have enough joy to encourage others, and have enough peace to stabilize their worries and fears!

> *"Wait and listen, everyone who is thirsty! Come to the waters; and he who has no money, come, buy and eat! Yes, come, buy [priceless, spiritual] wine and milk without money and without price [simply for the self-surrender that accepts the blessing]. Why do you spend your money for that which is not bread, and your earnings for what does not satisfy? Hearken diligently to Me, and eat what is good, and let your soul delight itself in fatness [the profuseness of spiritual joy]."* —Isaiah 55:1-2 AMP

God is El Shaddai, the God of more than enough. The excess that God releases to you is not to be wasted, but to pour out to others!

> *"The words of a [discreet and wise] man's mouth are like deep waters [plenteous and difficult to fathom], and the fountain of skillful and godly Wisdom is like a gushing stream [sparkling, fresh, pure, and life-giving]."* —Proverbs 18:4 AMP

No one can manufacture water as fresh as what God can give to you.

So many times when we receive an overflow of God's blessings, spiritually or naturally, we have a tendency to think, "Whew! I really needed that. Now if I can just hang onto this!"

I've watched as people so full of God stumble out of services filled with joy and courage, carefree and over-flowing with love, but emanating from them was, "Please don't talk to me or interrupt my party. I needed this touch from God and I just want to hang onto it." But the truth is, you will never keep it by holding onto it. The only way to preserve it is to give it away!

You can read the story in John 4 about Jesus going out of His way to visit Samaria and in particular the woman at the well. Let me read between the lines for you: Jesus was tired and hungry. He sat to rest while His friends insisted that they go get Him something to eat. In the meantime at the well, a Samaritan woman came by and Jesus asked her to get Him a drink. She was amazed that He, a Jew, even spoke to her who was considered "low-life." She was about to experience an encounter with the only One that could satisfy her life. She knew all too well that He was not just another man. Jesus knew she had been with five men and Jesus cut through her pain in acknowledging that fact to her. She challenged Him, as we all so often do, asking Him questions that skirted the real issues. When He told her point blank that if she knew who He was, she'd ask Him for a drink, she found it hard to understand from where the waters would come. She didn't realize that He was the Bread of Life, and Living Water. Jesus, anointed to open blind eyes, opened hers that day. So thrilled at her encounter, she ran to tell others of this man who knew all about her, but never condemned her. As she left, she dropped the water pot she had been holding and with it the old way of satisfying her thirst.

By the time the disciples returned, Jesus was not hungry anymore. Where did He get lunch? He abruptly said, "My meat is to do the will of the Father...I have meat that the world knows not of." Could it be that God is creating an appetite in us that cannot be satisfied by what we take in, but only by what we can give out?

## CHAPTER TWELVE

# THIS IS IT? OR IS THIS THAT?

*"This is [the beginning of] that which was spoken through the prophet Joel: And it shall come to pass in the last days, God declares, that I will pour out of My Spirit out upon all mankind..."* —Acts 2:16-17 AMP

When it comes to the revival for which we are all praying and anticipating, we tend to expect a moment in time when, like on the day of Pentecost, a mighty rushing wind will come. However, by Acts 2 the disciples had already come to the conclusion this wasn't "it." This was just the beginning of "that!"

Revival will have a beginning, but should have no end. As God is pouring out His Spirit, there is no doubt that believers everywhere are experiencing a fresh encounter with Jesus. For others, they realize that although they had received the Holy Spirit baptism at some point in their Christian lives, somehow they missed the fire and now they are experiencing a fire that cleanses, purges, and leaves them ablaze with a zeal for God. Some describe it as a spiritual awakening. It has been like they suddenly awakened to a purpose or destiny giving them a reason for living!

Acts 3:19 speaks to those whose hearts had once been given to God saying, "turn your hearts back to God, that your sins might be erased, blotted out and wiped clean." It is obvious that sin can delude us into thinking that we are serving God, when in reality we are way off course. When the light of God's glory comes, it wakes us up and shakes us to the truth. It is obvious that willful rebellion in our lives indicates a need to change, but is it possible that things as simple as following our own agenda, attempting to remedy our own problems, living life for our own purposes and getting weighed down with the cares of this world, or being critical and judgmental could be enough to get us off course and demand a turning back?

I believe that the lights are coming on for Christian believers who are hungering for a move of God. God is busy at work in the vineyard of our hearts and He is breaking up the fallow, hardened ground and bringing us to repentance with godly sorrow. It is a deep work of the Spirit. We can only thank God that He loves enough to tell us the truth in order to change us.

Revival is not an option, but an absolute necessity. As long as you can live without it, you will, but, if you will cry out with the psalmist David, in Psalm 85:6 "Wilt Thou not revive us again...?" God will hear your cry, and do just that! Charles Finney once said that every born-again, Spirit-filled believer needs revival every four to six weeks and you may be long overdue!

Once you have tasted the righteousness you have hungered and thirsted for (a place of sensing you are so "right" with God, clean and forgiven) and experienced the breath of God that restores and recovers your life from a gasping condition (where cares and the deceitfulness of riches, lusts for other things, has choked you for so long you found it hard to breathe), you'll never want to live without it again! Maybe you are just doing all the right things simply because you knew you should, but suddenly a breath of fresh air moves into your prayer life and you're not praying because you ought to, loving because you should, studying because you want another revelation, but there is just nothing you'd rather do! You find that there is joy in the house of prayer, and you are that house! You love not because you should, but because it is an overflow of being so securely loved. You find yourself studying not to be spiritual, but because you find sustenance in feeding on every word that comes out from the mouth of God. You are waiting. You long for His presence, not because you don't know where to go or what to do, but because you enjoy being with the One you love so deeply, drawing strength in His presence. You don't need to go anywhere or do anything else to be satisfied. Once revived again and having experienced the richest measure of His divine presence, you go on with a purpose, like Jesus did, doing good, healing all who are oppressed of the devil (Acts 10:38).

God is getting His church ready. It's taking a good spiritual house cleaning, but it is imperative that we be clean, pure vessels He can pour through in these last days. We all want a genuinely pure move of God in our churches, in our communities, and in our nation, but the move of God will only be as pure as the vessels it pours through. May our prayer be, "Bring change Lord, and let it begin in me!"

Acts 3:19 says, "Repent ye therefore, and be converted, that your sins may be blotted out, then the times of refreshing shall come from the presence of the Lord (KJV)." There will be times of refreshing in the presence of the Lord and that refreshing is vital for the days ahead. Notice God's Word says, "times" not "time." We must learn to come often to God's presence to be cleansed, restored and refreshed. In His presence is fullness of joy and pleasures forevermore. As the days ahead grow increasingly sober, we must know how to draw joy from the well of salvation (Isaiah 12:3) for His joy is our strength (Nehemiah 8:10).

## CHAPTER THIRTEEN

# EVER-FILLED AND EVER-READY

*"Therefore be imitators of God [copy Him and follow His example] as well-beloved children [imitate their fathers].*
—Ephesians 5:1 AMP

As imitators of God, we can learn His ways by simply watching the life of Jesus. He relinquished the ability to do anything apart from God. By His own admission, He did only what He saw the Father do and spoke only what He heard the Father speak. How simple. How profound. How entreating. He knew what He was here to do. He came with purpose—to destroy the works of the devil (I John 3:8).

He stood in the synagogue with a divine sense of destiny when He unrolled the scroll, and revealed His identity...

*"The Spirit of the Lord is upon Me, because He hath anointed Me to preach the gospel to the poor; He hath sent Me to heal the brokenhearted, to preach deliverance to the captives, and recovering of sight to the blind, to set at liberty them that are bruised, To preach the acceptable year of the Lord."*  —Luke 4:18-19 KJV

Jesus is the first fruit of many brethren, walking this destiny before us and showing us how to do it. We watch and learn as He arose early and continually pulled Himself apart throughout His busy days to seek the Father and stay in step with His purpose. He wasn't to be distracted, caught in offense, or discouraged when rejected. He stayed with His assignment, knowing what He was here to do and doing it. He moved daily from that place of prayer to a place of power and gave clear directions to the disciples that they were to do the same.

When He left, He gave them authority to do the works He had done. Then, most importantly, He sent them to a place to wait for the power to be what He had called to them be. They were to provide the container, an empty one, for the Holy Spirit to fill. The filling would provide for the spilling.

As they freely received, they could freely give. Lives touched by grace could extend grace to others. Those whose broken lives were healed would have the compassion to reach out to those still hurting. As they received comfort and encouragement, they would go in turn and release the same to others. God could spill His glory over the earth through containers who had chosen to be purged and cleansed. Just as foretold by the prophet in Joel 2:28, God is pouring out His Spirit on all flesh in this hour. Where we see a trickle now, there is soon to be a deluge.

When the promise of the Holy Spirit to come had been given and the instructions to tarry for this unknown event were to be carried out, one hundred twenty people abandoned the business of their lives, determined to wait for this power to be witnesses (Acts 1:8). It wasn't more instruction, but power to become what God had called them to be.

Then suddenly, like a mighty rushing wind, the Holy Spirit came with tongues like fire, joy infusing their soul. By the time they hit the streets, people surmised that they were drunk. They were so full of the power of God that they could not be contained in the upper room. They were bold. They were happy. They prophesied of things to come and soon they were moving about doing the works of Jesus. It was a wave of God's glory with signs that were making people wonder. The on-lookers could not resist the wisdom and eloquence with which these men spoke. The people who observed them knew that these men were not scholars, yet their words were such that they pricked their hearts!

More than three thousand were added to the church in a single day. They were threatened and told in no uncertain terms to stop this chaos of preaching with power and demonstration. But their response was, "You will have to decide for yourself if it is right to obey God or man. As for us, we can't help but tell!"

They had been so filled that the overflow was inevitable. They weren't trying, honestly. They just couldn't help it! I know exactly how they felt, having been so filled with the power of the Holy Spirit that I just couldn't help but weep, laugh, or shout praises to God!

The filling of the Holy Spirit meant spilling God's presence into the streets, to the highways, and byways. It provided living water for others who were thirsty. Soon, many others believed and *"the Lord added to the church daily such as should be saved"* (Acts 2:47 KJV).

However, this was not the end to this filling business. It became a regular practice of those who were spilling to return unto their own company of believers. Despite threats, they lifted their hands, praising God, and the place they were assembled was shaken and they were all filled, diffused with God's power, and headed back out of those four walls to be carriers of the glory, and spilled some more! (See Acts 4)

I used to think that when I read of God's glory covering the earth as the waters cover the seas, that some kind of mist would drop from heaven like a blanket to convince the whole world there was a God in heaven, and His presence would be known. Now, I see an even greater picture. The latter temple will be more glorious than the former. Since we are called the temple of the Holy Spirit, I believe we will be the containers of God's glory, carrying it throughout the earth, spilling into places, circumstances, and people's lives as we go.

It was about forty years after the outpouring of the Holy Spirit on the day of Pentecost when Ephesians 5:18 was written. Paul admonished the church not to be drunk with wine, but to be ever filled and ever stimulated with the power of the Holy Spirit. Being *ever filled* kept the believers *ever ready* to spill.

He gave them a simple recipe for staying filled. If there was no crowd gathered in praise or no prayer meeting going on; if their company was nowhere to be found, they could speak to themselves and one another in psalms, hymns, and spiritual songs, making melody in their heart to the Lord. They could create their own fueling station by lifting their voices and speaking of His glory and talking of His power.

Being filled is a continuing process. If we are doing what we were created to do, we are providing the vessels through a yielded life that God can fill with the richest measure of His own divine presence, and pour life through us to a hurting world.

## CHAPTER FOURTEEN

# ARE WE THERE YET?

I can still remember as a child being sandwiched between two older brothers in the back seat of a station wagon and asking, "Where are we going? Are we there yet? How long until we get there?" Sometimes, sandwiched in the pews of our churches, we can ask the same questions. It is hard to know when you've arrived if you don't know where you are going!

The truth is, we are on a journey and our Father definitely knows where He is taking us. Our path is growing brighter and brighter and we are headed not to paved highways, but off the beaten road, into the fields of harvest. I heard someone recently say that if you are looking for Jesus, He is not on the cross, He is out in the fields of harvest. You will find Him there!

We are far enough down the road now to look back and see where this outpouring has taken us. It is sending us to the streets, the highways, and byways, as it did on the days of Pentecost.

In Ft. Worth, Texas, it has taken our church to the city streets of their Jerusalem, ministering hands on to the inner city of Ft. Worth, but also to the ends of the earth with 24-hour Christian television, penetrating the nation of Uganda with the good news of Jesus Christ. In Romania, it has taken the church from their missions compound to the gypsy camps, building homes for people who have known no more than a cardboard box. In Saskatchewan, Canada, where temperatures plummet to 30 and 40 degrees below zero wind chills on winter mornings, 200 to 300 believers gather in the early hours to be filled again before reaching out to the native Indians whose lives have been bound by alcohol and drug addiction. In Decatur, Texas, the revival stirred the church to reach out to the youth in their community. In Brockton, Massachusetts, it poured the congregation into their community, sponsoring special events where 2,000 to 3,000 people would attend and hear the Gospel preached through innovative music, games, and prizes.

It was during a six week extended revival at Jubilee Family Church, in western Massachusetts that the congregation there experienced a powerful outpouring of the fire of God that touched their young people first...laughing, crying, being pinned to the floor. These teens, in a drunken stupor had to be carried out of services, only to be brought back by astonished parents who said their once sullen, quiet, lukewarm children were now reading their Bibles and praying fervently. It moved from teens to adults who experienced restored marriages, deliverances from harmful habits, as well as physical and emotional healings. Then the fresh hunger for God and passion for His Word prevailed. It spilled into the streets with their Heart Beat on the Street summer outreach program, and continues now through short-term missions trips where miracles are abundant and conversions have been dramatic. Because of the demonstration of God's fire Latin American pastors, many from conservative backgrounds, have become hungry for the Baptism of the Holy Spirit and received this gift with open hearts.

In all these communities and many others, it is moving the church outside their four walls to touch others they might never have reached had they not been filled to overflowing. Revival is for the church! Awakening is for the nations. God knows what He is doing...will you not make room for it?

*Let's pray together right now. Lord, I know there is so much more of You than I have experienced. Please stir my appetite to hunger for Your word, and times in Your presence. I know You are always with me and ever present, but there are times when I don't give attention to You – to Your leading, to Your voice. I'm asking You to transform my life and use me for Your purposes in the earth. I choose to be a vessel, a container of Your glory, so that others will experience Your love through me.*

*End Times, Blend Times*
*Blending the Spirit and the Word*
*What we've seen, with what we've heard.*

*Stepping in deeper, over our heads*
*Riding the river, raising the dead.*
*Restoring to life, wherever we go*
*Living and moving in a Holy Ghost flow.*

*Following God's heart, discerning His mind,*
*Being in the right places, at the right times.*
*It's the life of the Spirit, and all who abide*
*Can move in this river, just hang on for the ride!*

# HOW TO BE FILLED
# WITH THE HOLY SPIRIT

*"You're blessed when you've worked up a good appetite for God. He's food and drink in the best meal you'll ever eat."* — Matthew 5:6 THE MESSAGE BIBLE

Are you hungry to be filled to overflowing with the power of the Holy Spirit? Acts clearly tells us it is a promised gift to you, and your children and all who would receive (Acts 2:39). You will not be denied. Luke 11:11 (KJV) says, "If a son shall ask bread of any of you that is a father, will he give him a stone? Or if he ask a fish, will he for a fish give him a serpent?"

What is the purpose? You will receive power, ability, efficiency and might when the Holy Ghost comes upon you (Acts 1:8).

What about tongues? They were filled with the Holy Spirit and spoke with other tongues as the Spirit gave them utterance (Acts 2:4).

What is the purpose of tongues? To build yourself up, according to Jude 20. Romans 8:26 says, the Holy Spirit knows the mind and will of God. You don't know how to pray as you ought, but the Holy Spirit Himself does.

How do I speak with tongues? Remember, out of your belly it will flow. Syllables and expression unfamiliar to you will begin to "bubble up" on the inside of you as you pray to receive the Holy Spirit. Yield your tongue to the Holy Spirit and your heavenly language will begin to flow.

## Prayer to Receive

"Father God, I come to You today: hungry and thirsty for more of You. I want everything You have for me. I am so thankful that Jesus is the Lord of my life. I want to be filled to overflowing with the richest measure of Your divine presence. I want to be baptized with the Holy Spirit and speak with other tongues as the Spirit gives me utterance. I yield myself to You. I will speak with other tongues."

Now, begin to let those expressions out. Receive the gift of the Holy Ghost and continue to unwrap your gift daily, praying in the Spirit and keeping yourself built up by the power of the Holy Spirit. (See Jude 1:20)

Being filled with the Holy Spirit is not a one-time event. As you yield to the Spirit of God, you will be continually filled. When you are driving down the highway and see a "yield" sign, it means to give the right of way. In the same way, yielding to the Spirit of God means giving Him the right to lead and guide you. Romans 8:14 says all who are led by the Spirit of God are sons of God. Daily yield to the Holy Spirit speaking to yourself and others with psalms, hymns, and spiritual songs, making melody in your heart to the Lord (Ephesians 5:19). This will keep you "ever-filled." Living a life that is filled with God's Spirit, enables you to be used to SPILL God's love and healing power everywhere you go.

# END NOTES

1 Peterson, Karen S. "Research Shows Laughter Really Can Be a Boost for Your Health," *Tulsa World,* Nov. 10, 1996

2 "Research Confirms! Laughter Is Best Medicine," *The Orlando Sentinel*

3 Prophetic utterance given to me by the Lord, Summer 2000